BEING A PARENT

Parent Network

Based on the course *Understanding Children 1*
accredited by the National Open College Network

Written by Cath Johnstone

Consultant editor Sheila Munro

Hawthorn Press

PARENT
Network
Support & Education for Parenting

Being A Parent Copyright © 1999 Parent Network
2 Winchester House, 11 Cranmer Road, London, SW9 6EJ.
Parent Enquiry Line; 0171 735 1214 [020 7735 1214]
Fax. 0171 735 4692 [020 7735 4692]
E-mail. info@parentnetwork.demon.co.uk
Co. no. 2018523 Charity no. 327136 Vat no. 421 6504 84

Published by Hawthorn Press,
Hawthorn House, 1 Lansdown Lane, Stroud, Gloucestershire, GL5 1BJ
Tel. 01453 757040 Fax. 01453 751138

Cartoons by Viv Quillin
Illustrations by Paul Fisher Johnson
Cover photograph by Genna Naccache
Cover design by Patrick Roe, Southgate Solutions Ltd
Edited by Matthew Barton
Design and Typesetting by Frances Fineran of Hawthorn Press and Patrick Roe of Southgate Solutions Ltd
First edition, 1999
Printed by Redwood Books, Trowbridge, Wiltshire

Acknowledgements and permissions
Grateful acknowledgements for the poem 'Kids' by Spike Milligan, (published by Puffin/Spike Milligan Productions). Permission applied for.

A catalogue record for this book is available from the British Library
ISBN 1 869 890 817

Contents

AUTHORS AND THANKS

Being A Parent was written by Cath Johnstone and edited by Sheila Munro. It is based on the course *Understanding Children 1,* accredited by the National Open College Network and designed by members of the Parent Network 'pre-Parent-Link' group: Anna Clarke, Josephine MacLeod, Sheila Munro, Caroline Penney and Margaret Wainwright.

Cath Johnstone is a Parent Network facilitator and the mother of two children. She lives with her family in the Peak District.

THANKS ARE DUE TO …

- Ivan Sokolov and Jacquie Pearson, founders of Parent Network
- Monica Brooks who submitted a draft of the first two chapters
- Rachel Jenkins, Project Manager of Hawthorn Press
- all Parent Network facilitators who contributed ideas and suggestions
- all parents who were willing to talk about their experiences on the course
- all members of the Equal Opportunities group
- Parent Network staff: Sharon Ball, Ken Brown, Celia Dadzie, Ginny Dodd, Valerie Pelle and Roy Prockter
- members of the Parent Network Executive Committee
- all Parent Network trainers, facilitators, development workers and volunteers, who have given their time and energy to the movement for parent support and education
- all funders who support the work of Parent Network

ABOUT PARENT NETWORK

Parent Network is a national charity, founded in 1986, which aims to help parents get on well with their children. Courses are run by over 200 facilitators, who are parents themselves, in different parts of England, Scotland and Wales.

Parents who have taken Parent Network courses often report improvements in their children's behaviour and in family life. They say they have increased confidence and self-esteem. Parents are encouraged to continue meeting as self-help groups after the course has finished.

As part of our commitment to supporting parents, Parent Network is developing closer ties with other parenting and family organisations, especially with ParentLine, the national helpline for parents, and The National Stepfamily Association.

ABOUT PARENTLINE

ParentLine offers a vital and immediate link for parents and will complement the more comprehensive support provided by Parent Network courses. In addition, the pioneering work done by The National Stepfamily Association on listening to the views of children and young people will enhance our ability to support parents. The links will also ensure that Parent Network's work is relevant to anyone in a parenting role.

HOW TO FIND A COURSE

The Parent Enquiry line at Parent Network – 0171 735 1214 [020 7735 1214] – will give you a local contact who can let you know where courses are being run. If there is no course near you, you may be able to get a group together for one of our facilitators to come and run it.

You will usually have to pay something towards the course, and this varies around Britain depending on the circumstances – such as whether the course is run through a college, school or health authority. Concessionary places are available, and some courses are funded to allow parents to attend free of charge.

Course sessions are usually held weekly (total course hours: 14)

Parent Network

For information about courses:
0171 735 1214 [020 7735 1214]
e-mail: info@parentnetwork.demon.co.uk

ParentLine

 ParentLine

A national helpline which provides support and information to parents or anyone in a parenting role:
ParentLine: 0808 800 2222
Textphone: 0800 783 6783 (a phone service for people with hearing impairment)

Foreword

Being a parent can be one of the most wonderful things in the world. And, like gardening, it can also be a tough job, that requires skill, patience and stamina. As a parent myself, I know about some of the difficulties in bringing up children. Yet children, unlike packets of seeds, come without any growing instructions.

I consider this book and other Parent Network courses to have great value, because I believe that parents deserve all the help they can get – not just in dealing with major crises but with the day-to-day problems of family life.

I think that any mothers or fathers (or other relatives or carers) who try out this workbook and the 'Being A Parent' course will be doing themselves, and their children a big favour.

Good luck!

Alan Titchmarsh
TV and Radio Broadcaster, Author and Gardener

Introduction

Welcome to *Being A Parent*. This is the workbook which goes with Parent Network's *Being A Parent* course. It can be used on its own or as part of the course. This means you can work through it on your own or in a group with other parents.

This is a general guide for parents of children of all ages. We have used the term 'parents' to describe anyone who is in a parenting role. Families come in all sorts of shapes and sizes, and we wish to include all variations, from lone parents to stepfamilies-twice-removed to parents who are living apart from their children.

Although being a parent can be very rewarding, it can also be hard work. The aim of this book is to help parents and carers think about their role in bringing up children: what they find difficult, what they enjoy, and what support they might need. It aims to help parents feel more confident, and raise the self-esteem of their children.

Two of the most commonly heard remarks on Parent Network courses is 'I thought my child was the only one who behaved like that' or 'I thought I was the only parent to feel this way'! Parents feel reassured to know that others share the same kinds of problems and concerns.

The book recognises that most parents find it a struggle sometimes, and offers the hope that parents no longer need to suffer on their own. It gives ideas on meeting the needs of parents and children, understanding behaviour, and setting limits.

It also looks at the difference between assertive and aggressive behaviour, as well as the reasons why feelings matter.

In our diverse, multi-cultural society, there are many different beliefs about being a parent. There is no one, right way of bringing up children, and different things work for different people. You are encouraged to take from the book what works best for you and your children.

Above all, we recommend that you work through the exercises at your own pace, and be patient with yourself. In our many years' experience of running parenting courses, we know that these ideas really work; we also know that change can take time.

Good luck!

Cath Johnstone and Sheila Munro

CHAPTER 1   What it's really like being a parent

Before becoming a parent, did you ever think what it would be like? Many of us believed the ads, with pictures of happy, smiling mums and dads, and clean, cute babies. Sometimes the reality is very different!

In this chapter, we look at what being a parent is really like, what people find hard and what they enjoy, why parents matter, and how being on a parenting course can help.

Babies are hard work...

Babies are a joy, there is no doubt about that. And they can be very loveable. The joy they bring to parents can be like nothing else on earth.

But what the TV ads don't show is the *messy* side, the sleepless nights, the stress on parents' faces, the worry when a baby won't stop crying, the depression mothers sometimes suffer after the birth. Looking after babies is hard work, and can change our lives for ever.

A MOTHER: *Now she's crawling she's getting into everything – exploring and putting things in her mouth. Before, I could leave her in the pram. Now I have to watch her the whole time.*

And just when we think we know what we're doing, our baby starts to crawl and move around, and everything changes again. Then the baby becomes a toddler, the toddler becomes an infant, the infant becomes a school child – and before you know it you've got a teenager.

Each of these stages means a whole new set of things for parents to cope with, yet when we first became parents many of us never thought much beyond the stage of babyhood.

Of course, there are many rewards in bringing up children. Just the joy of seeing children take their first steps or say their first words, or sharing a warm, loving hug, can be wonderful. Children and parents give each other a lot of love.

One of the most important jobs in the world

Being a parent is one of the most important jobs in the world. It can also be one of the hardest, yet how many of us get any training for it? Most of us learn as we go, by trial and error and with little support.

A FATHER: *Being a parent has changed my life. It's made me see the world through the eyes of children. Not just my own children, but other people's as well, and when I hear anything on the news about children it touches me deeply.*

If the job of being a parent were advertised, it would probably read something like this:

> **WANTED: volunteer (unpaid) for**
> ***very demanding job.***
>
> **Would suit person with the following skills: teaching, cooking, running a household, sorting out arguments, nursing, solving all kinds of problems, giving advice, having eyes in the back of your head, juggling lots of different things at once. Applicant must be committed, flexible and patient, have energy, sense of humour and an understanding of children at different ages and stages. Night shifts are part of the job.**
>
> **No qualifications necessary.**
> **No training given but ample opportunity to learn on the job!**

Describing parenthood like that shows what a tall order it really is. Most of us have had no training in these skills, but are expected just to get on with it. It's no wonder many parents feel stressed, or worried about whether they are doing the job well enough.

Being a parent can be stressful

Life goes on, but it's not the same

Probably very few of us are fully prepared for the changes that take place in our lives when we first have children:

- we probably don't get enough sleep

- there's not enough time even to get basic jobs like cleaning the home done

- we may stop going out as much as we did before

- we may have strong feelings that we've hardly ever felt before

- if we have a partner, our relationship with him/her may change

A MOTHER: *One of the biggest things about being a parent is how committed you have to be. It's not like any other job I've done.*

Helping each other

Admitting what we find hard is an important step in getting the help or support we need. Whatever stage our children (or even grandchildren) are at, joining a parenting group can help, because it gives us the chance to talk about things with other parents or grandparents.

LIFE AS A PARENT

Think about the things that changed in your life when you had children. Talk about them with a friend, or write them down here. Then think about the questions below, or talk about them with a partner on the course.

What did you expect the job of a parent to be like? (Did you think about it?)

What changes have you found hardest to cope with?

Did you have any previous experience? (Such as looking after younger brothers or sisters)

What skills do you use in the job?

What skills, if any, do you need more of?

What do you think are the most important qualities for being a parent? (For example patience, being easy-going, sense of humour)

What help or support have you had?

What help or support would you like?

How might you find support?

How our job as a parent changes as our children grow

As our children grow our roles as parents change. This depends, of course, on the abilities – or disabilities – of the child. Here are some of the roles parents may play over the years:

When children are:	The parents' role will mostly be:
babies	caring, feeding, protecting from harm, giving love and affection
toddlers	caring and guiding, setting limits, helping them understand their world, picking up after a fall, keeping safe
in mid-childhood	caring and guiding, setting limits, teaching new skills, being a friend, someone they can talk to
adolescents	guiding, teaching, setting limits, being a friend and consultant (giving advice when asked)
adults	being a friend and consultant
parents	being a friend and consultant, offering support and a helping hand when needed
at all stages	giving love and support

Many parents find some of their children's stages easier than others. For instance, you might find dealing with a little baby quite easy, but a seven year old very difficult. Or the other way round.

Different kinds of families

There isn't one right way to bring up children. Western society has changed a lot over the past century and today families come in all shapes and sizes. You may:

- be part of a married couple

- be divorced and living with someone who has children from a previous relationship

- be a parent who only sees your children during holidays or at weekends

- have adopted a child or children

- be bringing up the kids on your own

- be living in an 'extended' family together with aunts, uncles and grandparents

- be part of a gay or lesbian couple who are bringing up children

- be one of several unrelated families living together in a community

Parents in any setting can do a good job of bringing up their children. Each kind of family has its own problems for parents and children to deal with. The most important thing is that parents love and care for their children.

Different cultures

There are parents of many different cultures, religions and ethnic backgrounds in Britain today. Many of us have our own ways of bringing up children and we come from all sorts of different backgrounds.

If you are doing this course in a group, you will probably find that different parents in the group have different ideas about what is best for their children. Being in a group gives parents the chance to talk about their lives and learn from each other's differences, and even disagree!

Being a parent can be tough

Being a parent can be tough, especially if we are bringing up children in a difficult situation. This might include any of the following: living in cramped or poor housing conditions, being unemployed or having a low income, having a serious illness or a disability in the family, working long hours, feeling alone or isolated, not having friends or family close by who can give help when you need it, living in Britain and not having English as your first language, or living in fear of violence or abuse.

Even people who do not have these sorts of difficulties often find being a parent really hard.

Use this space to write down the things you find difficult as a parent, or talk about them with a friend. Underline the hardest things.

What might make a difference? (If you like, pretend for a moment that you have a fairy godparent. What would you ask for that would make life easier for you as a parent? Be as outrageous as you like!)

Now write down one thing that you might be able to do or work on that could make a difference.

Being a parent's great fun too!

BUT not everything needs to seem like an uphill struggle, for being a parent or carer can also bring us a lot of pleasure! One of the aims of this book is to help parents get more enjoyment out of being a parent.

The joy of being a parent

The more we enjoy the job of being a parent, the more likely we are to bring up happy children.

Sometimes it's the little things that bring parents most joy, even when they are under a lot of stress. Not all parents enjoy all the things in this list, but most of us can find something we enjoy:

- having fun with our children

- watching our children play together (when they are getting on well!)

- feeling needed

- cuddles and kisses

- watching our children's faces when they are opening presents

- feeling proud of what our children do

- noticing new stages of development (the first smile, the first few steps, the first words)

- sharing bed-time stories

WHAT DO YOU ENJOY ABOUT BEING A PARENT?

Write here the things you like about being a parent, or talk about them with a friend. If you can't think of many to start with, you can add more during the course.

Parents matter

Our children are tomorrow's adults and we are often the most important people in their lives. What we do and say affects them.

Who knows what their child will become? Your two-year-old having a tantrum might end up an MP! Whatever lies in store for our children the job of raising them to take their place in the world is very important. We parents deserve to be appreciated more than we usually are. We are very valuable members of society.

Looking after ourselves

We matter, so it's important to look after ourselves as well as our children. Taking even a few minutes for ourselves every day can work wonders if we are feeling stressed, and can help us look after our children better.

It can be easy to feel guilty about taking time out from the chores, especially when those chores keep staring us in the face. It's a good idea to remind yourself that you'll do them better if you look after yourself as well.

You may like to have a go at the next exercise, which can take as little as five minutes.

A STRESS-FREE ZONE

Choose a time when you know your children are safe, when they're asleep, at school, or being well looked after. We suggest you switch off the TV or radio.

Sit somewhere comfortable and quiet, and close your eyes. Take a deep breath and let it out slowly – feel yourself sink more deeply into your seat.

Imagine yourself surrounded by a soft bubble that protects you.

Be aware of all the outside things and people that make demands on your life.

Now feel yourself gently making your bubble bigger, pushing back all these demands. All your concerns about money, your children, work can just wait.

Every time you breathe out make your bubble a bit larger until you feel really comfortable. Know that you can step out of the bubble whenever you need to, but for now just relax.

When you are ready, open your eyes and see your surroundings. Be aware of that bubble space you have created around you. Whenever you want to, go back into the bubble and relax.

Ground rules

If you are on a Parent Network course you will probably have agreed some ground rules with the other group members.

Ground rules are important because they make clear some of things we can expect from the group. They help to build trust and make the group a safer place. For instance, we can feel more comfortable talking about ourselves or our problems if we know that people will keep what we say to themselves, and not spread it around.

GROUND RULES

This space is for you to list the ground rules that have been agreed in your group. They may be added to as you go on.

CHAPTER 2   We're doing our best

Part 1

Many parents are bringing up children in difficult situations. But this does not stop them from loving and caring for their children as well as they can.

One of the most important things parents can do for their children is to help them feel good about themselves, or give them 'self-esteem'. Children who feel good about themselves get on better with others, are more co-operative, and enjoy life more.

Helping our children

Here are some of the most valuable things we can do for our children. Many of them help children build their self-esteem.

GIVE CHILDREN ATTENTION

This is one of the most important things any parent can give a child. Children need to know that they are important to us, and we can make them feel this just by enjoying being with them.

There are lots of ways to give attention, and many of them cost nothing, such as:

- spending time with them, just being with them, or hearing about their school day if they want to talk about it

- listening to them when they want to tell you something

- playing a game with them

- telling them a bit about your own day – but avoid putting your worries on them

A MOTHER: *I got a job that meant I didn't get nearly enough time with my children, so something had to go. I began to wonder how important it was to have all our clothes ironed to perfection, a habit I'd inherited from my mother. And how important was it that the flat was spotless? It's been hard, but I've changed my priorities – clothes are a bit crumpled and the flat's not so tidy, but at least I get time with the kids.*

It is good to know that one of the most important things for our children's happiness doesn't have to cost anything! Children tend to want more and more material things, which we may not be able to afford or may not want them to have. Attention is a gift we can give them every day, which shows them that they are important to us.

Children who don't get enough attention tend to behave badly in order to get it.

HUG THEM EVERY DAY

Human beings need physical affection. If your own parents did not hug you, you may feel feel uneasy hugging your children at first. Even teenagers need a hug sometimes.

LISTEN TO WHAT THEY WANT TO TELL YOU

One of the best things we can do for anybody is to listen to them. Listening to our children is another way of showing that they are important to us and that their thoughts and feelings matter.

LET THEM PLAY, BOTH ON THEIR OWN AND WITH OTHER CHILDREN

Playing is how children learn. Through play they learn how to use their bodies and minds, how to relate to other people. (There's more about play later in this chapter).

LET THEM DO THINGS FOR THEMSELVES

Doing things for themselves makes children confident, and gives them the chance to learn new skills and become independent. For instance, we could let a child pay for his/her own comic in the shop, or older children could make their own packed lunches. (We look more at this in chapter 6).

TRY NOT TO MAKE THEM DO THINGS BEFORE THEY ARE READY

But it is important to let children develop at their own speed. One child may be able to do up coat buttons by the age of three, whereas another might not manage it until the age of four or five.

If we put pressure on them to do things before they are ready, or compare them with others who can do things they cannot do yet, they are likely to lose confidence and feel bad about themselves.

If you have any worries about your children's development, their teacher or your health visitor will probably be able to help.

TALK WITH THEM OFTEN — EVEN BABIES

Children learn to talk by listening to us talk. They begin to make sense of language from the moment they are born, perhaps even when they are still in the womb, and can understand quite complicated things well before they can talk themselves. Talking to our children from birth onwards helps them in this learning, and lets them know they matter to us.

LET THEM CLIMB, SKIP AND RUN

Getting exercise helps children be healthy and develop well. Many disabled children can enjoy the chance to move around and get fresh air as much as other children.

Outdoor exercise is especially good, but if you don't have a park or garden nearby, having old furniture that children can climb or bounce on is ideal.

LET THEM ENJOY MUSIC AND SINGING

Most children love music. Even babies love being sung to and can be calmed by gentle music. The rhythms and rhymes of songs and music (such as nursery rhymes) are important in helping young children learn to talk. As they get older, listening to and playing music can be good ways of getting together with others and expressing themselves.

PRAISE THEM FOR WHAT
THEY DO WELL

Children need to get positive comments from their parents – this helps them feel positive about *themselves*. Praising even small achievements is helpful, for instance saying something like 'Well done, you're ready on time'. It's a good idea to *avoid* adding a criticism like 'but you look a mess', as this could wipe out the value of the praise.

ENJOY BOOKS
WITH THEM

We can help give our children a love of books by reading to them from when they are very small. Even just looking at books together and talking about the pictures is good. (If your child is visually impaired you can get 'hearing books' from most libraries.) As they grow older, you may enjoy working or playing on a computer with them as well.

You may already do many of these things.

Things we do well

Many of us have a little voice inside our head which criticises us, but which rarely notices when we do something well. This is a shame, because, just like our children, we too need to feel good about ourselves.

We may have a picture in our minds of what the 'perfect parent' is like – someone who would have no difficulty in getting the job in the advert on page 2. *But there is no such thing as the perfect parent.* We are all human. All of us have things we could learn and all of us have things we do well.

WHAT YOU DO WELL AS A PARENT

Think about the things that you do well as a parent. They could be very simple things like singing to your children, or taking them to the park. Or you may do some of the things in the list above. Write them down here or talk about them with a friend.

For example: *I like the way I let my children paint and draw.*

Appreciating yourself does not mean you are being 'big-headed'. It is just a matter of being honest with yourself and accepting that you have your own qualities, just like everyone else.

Noticing what we do well and giving ourselves regular pats on the back helps us feel good about ourselves. It can also make it easier for us to change the things we would like to change.

Listening

When our children have a problem, one of the best ways we can help is to listen. Just letting them get something off their chest often makes it seem less of a problem, and shows them that we care – even if we don't agree with their point of view.

Very often, the most useful way to listen is just to pay full attention to what the other person is saying, to keep quiet, and not to butt in with our own point of view. We can let them know that we are paying attention by nodding, and saying things like 'mmm' and 'oh'.

QUIET LISTENING EXERCISE

Do this with a friend or partner on the course, someone you feel at ease with.

Spend about five minutes talking about a problem that's worrying you at the moment. It could be anything you feel OK talking about – for example, something to do with your children, your job, the state of your neighbourhood, an argument you had with a friend or relative.

Ask your friend just to listen in silence, without making a comment or asking questions.

When the five minutes is up, talk to your friend about what it felt like to be listened to in this way. Ask your friend to share what it felt like to be the listener.

Then swap roles so that your friend talks about a problem and you listen.

Now practise quietly listening to your child or children.

Looking after ourselves

Our own and our children's happiness are closely linked. When children are happy it often helps their parents to be happy. When parents are feeling happy it often rubs off on their children.

Looking after ourselves might feel like a luxury that we can't afford. We can be so busy seeing to the needs of our families that we might forget about our own needs. But we cannot go on for ever looking after other people unless we recharge our own batteries from time to time.

A MOTHER: *I find doing a big shop with my twins in tow really stressful. When I get in I always make myself a drink and sit down for quarter of an hour before doing the putting away or anything else. The girls know they're not allowed to make any demands during that time. If ever I don't get that break I'm so ratty, so it's for their sake as well as mine that I need it.*

One of the best ways to look after yourself is to do something that you enjoy. It could be something as simple as taking a long bath or having 15 minutes with a good book at bed-time. Or it could be spending an evening with a friend, or signing up for a class in something you've always wanted to do. (Many colleges and community centres offer creche facilities to help parents of small children attend classes.)

What's important is that it is something you *enjoy,* rather than something you think you *ought* to do.

DOING SOMETHING JUST FOR YOURSELF

Talk with a friend or someone on your group about the things you enjoy doing just for you, not for other people. Write them down here.

Now make a deal with yourself to do at least one of these things during the next week. Then decide how you can do this (e.g. ask a friend, or your partner if you have one, to mind the children for an hour, so you can have a long, relaxing soak in the bath.) Remember, doing things for yourself is not selfish, unless you *only* think of your own needs all the time. If we want to do the best for our children we also need to do the best for ourselves.

CHAPTER 2   Children and Play

Part 2

Why children need to play

As well as being fun, play is one of the most important ways that children learn. From the moment they reach out to hit a rattle as a baby, to the time they start going to discos or the bowling alley as teenagers, they are learning about themselves, their world and how to behave in it through play.

As parents, it's easy to look at young children building sand-castles, dressing up, or getting messy with paint and glue, and think they're 'just playing'. But this 'just playing' is vital for our children's development. If we don't let them play, it could stop them growing up into happy, self-confident adults.

As children go through different stages of development, different types of play are important.

Below we look at some different types of play, why they are important for our children, and how we can help them get the most from playing.

PLAYING WITH OTHER CHILDREN

At all ages, it's important for our children to spend time with other children. Whatever they play, they learn skills like sharing with others, co-operating, standing up for themselves and sorting out quarrels.

MESSY PLAY

Childhood is a messy business, right from the beginning. Some of us find dealing with mess and untidiness one of the hard things about being a parent. But playing with things like water and sand is the one of the best ways for young children to learn about the world and develop their skills.

Messy play gives hours of fun and can be completely free. All we need is a kitchen sink, or washing-up bowl on the floor, some water and common kitchen items such as beakers and sponges. For playing with sand a bucket or large tray, plastic spoons or spades, a sieve and some plastic containers are enough.

Always make sure you supervise young children's play

Young children cannot play with sand and water without making a mess. So it's important not to make them feel bad about it. If we get them to help tidy up at the end, especially if we make that into part of the game, we're encouraging good habits from an early age, and teaching that mess is no problem because it can get cleaned up.

CREATIVE ACTIVITIES

Young children love painting, drawing, making models out of scrap or with playdough. These activities encourage their imagination, help develop skills (e.g. holding paintbrushes and manipulating playdough), and can let them express their feelings. Again, they needn't be expensive. All sorts of scrap materials can be used for making models – cartons and boxes, yoghurt pots and so on. Playdough can be made at home (see appendix).

Children learn more by trying out things for themselves than by us telling them. For example they can find out what red and blue will make by mixing it themselves.

As well as enjoying doing these things on their own, children get a lot from us joining in. It can be fun for us as well!

As they get older, many children still enjoy being creative.

PLAYING 'LET'S PRETEND'

When children pretend to be different people in games, they are often copying the things adults do and say. In this way they start to learn about different roles in life – for instance, being a mum or dad – and about social values – for instance when they play a 'baddy' or a 'goody'. This sort of play is important well into the school years.

Dressing up is an important part of pretending. A dressing-up box can be put together very cheaply using our own old clothes, scraps of material and bits and pieces from jumble sales.

PLAYING WITH DOLLS
AND MODELS

This sort of play helps children develop hand skills (dressing a doll needs hands and eyes to work together), and is similar to 'let's pretend', allowing children to try out different roles and feelings.

COUNTING AND
SORTING GAMES

When children count, sort things into groups, measure and so on as part of their play, they are really doing early maths and learning skills that will help them at school. Many of these sorts of activities, including doing puzzles, also help develop the skills they need later when they begin to learn to read. Children can get very involved in these sorts of activities, so they can also help them learn to concentrate.

Free play

Children will get the most from all these activities if we let them find their own ways of doing things. Telling them what to do all the time will only cramp their style.

These examples are just a few of the almost endless ways that young children learn through play. Whenever they are playing, they are learning something, even though we may not be able to work out what it is! When they come to more formal learning at school, they will have a good start if they've done plenty of playing.

PLAYING

What kind of play did you enjoy as a child?

What do your children enjoy now?

What do you think is good about this kind of play?

Is there any play activity that you find hard?

If so, what might help to make it easier?

Older children

As children get older, different sorts of play become more important. Older children often enjoy board games, cards and paper and pencil games (such as hangman and noughts and crosses). These are a good way for people of different ages to play and enjoy being together, for example children and grandparents, or older and younger children.

Computer games of course feature strongly in many children's lives these days – but for health reasons it is better if parents don't let them spend too long on this at any one time.

For lots of children, playing after school is important, just as doing something relaxing is important for many adults when they get in from work. Sometimes children might need physical play to let off steam and get exercise, other times a quiet activity will help them unwind.

Children 'grow out' of different sorts of play at their own speed. If a child is still enjoying 'let's pretend' or messy play after his/her friends have moved on to other ways of playing, it's a sure sign that she or he still has things to learn from that sort of play.

It's important not to make children feel embarrassed or bad about this, for instance by telling them they're being babies. As long as there are opportunities to do other things children usually move on when they are ready, at the right time for them. However, if you are worried, it is a good idea to talk to an expert – e.g. a teacher or health worker

'Play' for the teens

Teenagers' activities are not usually thought of as 'play', but they are still learning from what they do. When they go to a disco with a group of friends, they are enjoying dancing and learning about forming relationships. Trying out different styles (dressing up!), changing groups of friends – these sorts of activities help teenagers find out where they fit in and become more independent.

Learning happens all the time

It's not just at school that children learn. Even when they seem to be just 'mucking about' and letting off steam, all kinds of learning can be going on. To sum up we can say that play is just as important for our children as our work is for us – though perhaps more enjoyable! Playing well and happily early on helps them get the most out of life later.

CHAPTER 3 Why children behave the way they do

Have you ever wondered *why* people behave the way they do? Why do babies cry? Why do children pick fights? Why do teenagers rebel?

The bottom line is that people – both adults and children – *do what they do in order to get what they need.*

We all have needs

We all have needs. Some needs are basic – if they were not met, we would die. Others are not so basic, but are still important for our well-being; if they are not met, we might get mentally or physically ill, or have problems in our relationships with other people. Or we might have a deep feeling of unhappiness in our lives.

SOME
HUMAN NEEDS

food	love
drink	affection
shelter	to express feelings
warmth	approval
safety from danger	attention of others
freedom from disease	feeling good about ourselves
physical affection –	mental stimulation
i.e. cuddles & hugs	sleep

Babies, children and adults all share these needs

Babies and children need adults to help them get what they need. But adults don't automatically know what a child needs at any one time. That is why children behave in different ways: to get their needs met.

For example, when babies are hungry and need to be fed, they cry. When children are hurt and need to be comforted, they cry.

Of course, a baby doesn't have to *learn* to cry when it's hungry or hurt. Crying is an instinct, a way in which the baby tries to get its needs met. Because a new-born baby's cry is almost impossible for most adults to ignore, it is very well designed to get a parent to try to give the baby what it needs.

A FATHER: *I heard about some research that was done by a siren manufacturer into what are the most attention-grabbing sounds. A human baby's cry came top. Listening to Sarah I'm not surprised.*

As children grow, they learn new ways of getting their needs met. For instance, instead of crying, they learn to ask for food when they're hungry, and eventually to make something to eat themselves.

Here are some examples of how children might try to get their needs met:

• wanting to sit on someone's knee – need for affection

• climbing on us when we're trying to talk to a friend – need for attention

• refusing to wear the clothes we've got out – need to be more independent

• wanting us to stay with them until they get to sleep – need for security

• showing us what they've done – need for approval

• wanting to join in a game we're playing with our other children – need to feel fully part of the family

• doing things with their friends that you've told them not to do – need to fit in with their friends

HOW YOUR CHILDREN TRY TO GET WHAT THEY NEED

Here are some examples of how children behave to meet their needs

Child's behaviour: drawing on the walls
Need might be: to get attention *or* to be creative

Child's behaviour: refusing to keep their room tidy
Need might be: to show independence by doing it their own way *or* to fit in with friends

Child's behaviour:
Need might be:

Child's behaviour:
Need might be:

Now think of some different needs that could be behind the following:

Behaviour: toddler splashing water all over the floor
Need might be:
or:
or:

Behaviour: sister hassling an older brother to let her play with him and his friends
Need might be:
or:
or:

Behaviour: teenager taking drugs
Need might be:
or:
or:

Now think of some ways your own children behave and
what needs they might be trying to meet:

Child's behaviour:
Need might be:

Child's behaviour:
Need might be:

Of course, it isn't always possible for parents to meet all their children's needs! One of the hardest things about being a parent is trying to sort the different needs of different family members – perhaps all at the same time! As parents we can't always meet everyone's needs.

Different ways of getting needs met

The ways children find to satisfy their needs often do not cause problems for anyone. However, sometimes children learn ways to meet their needs that do cause problems for those around them. For instance:

- A child comes in from school hungry, and whines until we give him or her something to eat

- A child needs attention, so makes a lot of noise when we're on the phone

- A teenager needs to show independence, so goes to the pub under age, having been told clearly that this isn't allowed. (This could also be because of the need to fit in with friends.)

Although we may not *agree* with how our children are trying to meet a need, it is good to remember that their behaviour can tell us about a real need that they have.

We can help our children behave in ways that don't cause problems by offering them different ways to meet their needs. We can teach our three-year-old to ask and to take turns, instead of fighting another child to get a toy. If an older child whines when asking for something, we can ask him or her to use a normal voice and say what s/he wants. Children are in fact less likely to whine all the time when we give them what they need.

Is it really misbehaviour?

When our children do things we don't like it can be easy to think of what they've done simply as good or bad behaviour. But what someone does can be OK or not, depending on the situation, the time, the place, the person doing it and how we feel at the time.

For instance, we might feel alright about our children playing music loudly at 4.00 in the afternoon, but not at 1.00 in the morning. Tipping a drink onto the floor might be OK from a baby who hasn't learned not to, but a different matter from a nine-year-old if it's done on purpose. If we're feeling tired and stressed, children having a rough and tumble in the same room might be hard to take, whereas at another time it would be fine.

So instead of seeing behaviour as simply good or bad, it can be more useful to think about whether or not it's a problem at that moment.

THE THINGS OUR CHILDREN DO

Think about when you might find it alright or not alright for children to behave in the following ways. It might be to do with WHO is doing it, the situation they are in, WHERE or WHEN they are doing it, or how you are feeling at the time.

Shouting and screaming:

     alright:

     not alright:

Punching and kicking someone:

     alright:

     not alright:

Sitting in their room reading:

     alright:

     not alright:

Standing on the dining table:

     alright:

     not alright:

Finding out the needs

It's not always easy to know what children need when they are behaving a certain way, because they don't always know themselves. Sometimes listening can help us find out. But even if we can't work it out, just realising that they are behaving that way to try to meet their needs can help us understand our children better.

Needs are different from wants

It would be easy to believe that children *need* all sorts of material things. We are bombarded with advertising messages suggesting that our children will never be happy unless we buy them the latest computer game, a particular bike or whatever is the latest craze.

As parents we can easily feel like failures because we can't or don't want to provide everything our children want. But what they want is not always the same as what they *need*.

A FATHER: *My son was putting together a model dinosaur he'd bought. I could hear him getting cross, muttering under his breath, gradually getting louder. I went and sat with him, not saying anything. He was quite frustrated by now, obviously having a problem with it. After a while I said 'Annoyed?', and he blurted out 'Oh, Dad! I need some help with it!'*

I badly wanted a really expensive coat that I just couldn't afford. When I thought about it I knew I didn't need *a new coat, but I realised that all my clothes were getting shabby, and I needed to feel better about myself when I went out. I went to the Nearly New shop and got a load of good, smart clothes for a fraction of the price of the coat. I feel fine about myself now, and don't particularly want the coat any more.*

Although wants and needs are not the same, they are linked. For instance, when children *want* the most up-to-date fashion clothes, it can be because they *need* to fit in with their friends. Or if an adult *wants* to go out for a walk, it could be that he or she *needs* some exercise, or relaxation, or time to think through a problem.

Always giving in to a child's immediate want can lead to problems later. For instance, a toddler might have a tantrum because he can't have the toy he wants. If we then give him the toy because he's making such a fuss, he may learn that tantrums are a good way of getting his needs met. Then next time he wants something, he has a tantrum.

This is not to say that it is wrong to give children what they want; but that sometimes we can meet their needs in other ways.

Talking and labelling

As parents we often want to tell our children what we think of their behaviour. When they do things that cause problems, either for themselves or other people, it's our job to teach them what they could do instead.

Labels are shortcut ways of saying what we don't like. We often use them, especially if we are angry, because they are quick and easy. In the phrases below, the words in bold are all labels:

You **naughty** boy .

How **stupid!**

She's always been **mean**.

You're so **bossy.** Leave her alone.

Don't be such a **wimp.**

When we use labels to describe children several things can happen:

- children can believe the labels and feel hurt and bad about themselves

- children might start to act more and more as the labels suggest, because they start to believe that it's expected of them

- children might not understand what it is we want them to do

When we want to comment on what our children are doing, we can avoid using labels by talking about the *behaviour itself* rather than labelling the *child*.

Here are some examples:

Instead of 'You're so untidy' we could say 'You left your bag and coat on the floor'

Instead of 'What an idiot!' we could say 'I don't think you understand what I mean'

Instead of 'You're rude' we could say 'I don't like it when you swear.'

Think of what you might say about a child's behaviour without labelling the child in these situations:

A child is refusing to let his brother have a go on the swing.

At a meal time, the child's food is going on the floor.

A child is playing games instead of getting ready for school.

A teenager took the car without asking.

A child's new coat got torn by climbing a tree.

When we describe what the child *did* rather than label the *child,* the child is more likely to understand what it is we don't like. If children know that it's what they are *doing* not who they *are* that's the problem, they are likely to feel better about themselves and more likely to feel able to change their behaviour.

Getting our own needs met

As we have seen, parents often put their own needs aside to look after their families. We may forget to eat because we're too busy cooking for the children. We may not take any time for ourselves because we feel bogged down with our job or with housework. But our needs are important too.

Getting to know our own needs and beginning to get them met is important both for ourselves and our children.

GETTING YOUR OWN NEEDS MET

Are there any areas of your life that you are not happy with?

Can you say what you need, which would make you feel better?

How could you begin to get what you need?

Who could you ask for help?

It can be painful to realise that you might not have been getting your needs met. If you find it hard to think about, we suggest you start with small things, moving on to bigger things later.

When we are getting what we need, we are usually happier and more able to look after our children and help them get what they need.

Getting our own needs met

He's definitely angry about something

CHAPTER 4   Feelings Matter

Being a parent is an emotional business. Children's emotions can be very strong, and difficult for us to deal with sometimes. Children also have the knack of 'pushing our buttons' that is, setting off our own emotions.

Why are feelings important?

Knowing what to do to help our children with their feelings can be one of the hardest parts of being a parent. Yet our feelings are an important part of who we are. They can tell us about our needs and what's good for us. Sometimes their messages are very important. Here are some examples of what our feelings could tell us:

• **FEAR** can tell us when we're in real danger

• **ANGER** can mean that we don't accept what's happening to us

• feeling **LONELY** could tell us that we need more contact with other people

• feeling **HAPPY** usually tells us that what we're doing is right for us

As we grow up, we sometimes learn that our feelings, or some of them, are 'wrong' or 'unimportant'. Being told 'there's no need to get upset' or 'you shouldn't be angry' teaches us that our feelings are wrong. Being told 'I don't care if you're upset' tells us that our feelings don't matter. Or, if our parents did not show their emotions, we are likely to grow up thinking that it's not OK to show feelings.

If we come to believe that our feelings are wrong, that they don't matter, or that they shouldn't be seen, we may learn to take no notice of them, or to hide them. There can be several problems with this:

- the feelings could build up and explode later

- we might not find out what the feelings could tell us about ourselves or our situation

- we may start to feel bad about ourselves or guilty for feeling the way we do

- feelings that are buried for long periods can make us ill in the end. Anger turned inwards can later lead to depression

We can help both ourselves and our children by learning to accept that feelings are natural, even the uncomfortable ones.

Feelings are natural

YOUR CHILDREN'S FEELINGS

Think about the feelings that your children show.

How do they show their various feelings? (For example, what do they do to show they're angry, bored, hurt etc?)

Which of their feelings do you feel OK about?

Which of them do you *not* feel OK with?

How do you tend to react when your children show strong feelings? (For example, if they scream when they're angry, what do you do or how do you feel?)

Do your reactions to your children's feelings change depending on how you are feeling at the time? (For instance, some people find it harder to hear about another person's happy feelings when they are feeling stressed.)

Some feelings are harder to cope with than others

Feelings can be painful. This is true both of feelings we have ourselves and of feelings other people show us. Very often the feelings we find difficult to cope with, either in ourselves or in our children, are the *ones that we were not allowed to show when we were little.*

For example, if we were told off for getting angry, the chances are that will we grow up feeling bad, perhaps guilty, when we do feel angry. Or if we were always expected to be cheerful and not to appear miserable, we might find that we get annoyed when our own children are feeling fed up.

lonely

bored

flustered

relaxed

happy

eager

jealous

embarrassed

miserable

hurt

confused

sad

proud

peaceful

contented

irritated

satisfied

anxious

relieved

✻◆✳✻ ◆☆

angry

frustrated

afraid

serious

uncomfortable

These are just some of the feelings both adults and children can have

Feelings change

Human emotions are not fixed. Our feelings can change quickly and often.

Babies' and toddlers' emotions can change dramatically from one moment to the next. For example a toddler might be playing happily one minute and suddenly burst into tears because of a door slamming. Or a young baby might be crying hard one minute and smiling and gurgling the next, when its interest is caught by a colourful toy or a rattle. This is very natural and normal.

Children's emotional reactions also change as they learn about their world. For instance, babies may be distressed when their carer leaves the room, but once they learn that she or he will come back, they no longer get upset.

Adults' feelings can change often too, although they tend not to show their feelings in the same way because they have learned to hide and control them more.

One person can have different feelings about the same thing at different times. For example, we may feel OK about our children's noise and mess one day but find it too much to cope with the next.

YOUR OWN FEELINGS

What are the feelings you have most often? (You could use the picture on page 38 to help name your feelings, or you might have other feelings that are not shown in the picture.)

How do you show your different feelings? (For instance, if you feel happy, do you sing? Laugh a lot? Cuddle your children more than usual? If you feel angry do you shout? Speak through clenched teeth?)

Are there any feelings that you don't like to show? (For instance, you might not like people to see you cry if you're sad.)

Which of your feelings do you feel alright about having? (In other words, even though the feeling itself might be uncomfortable, you know that it's OK to feel that way.)

Which of your feelings do you feel bad about having? (For example, you might feel that it's not all right to get angry or to feel jealous.)

Some people find it difficult to talk about their feelings. Others are not always aware of what their feelings are. If you don't feel like talking about your feelings in the group, you don't have to. You may want to take time to explore this another time, with someone you trust.

Letting our children have their feelings

Children need to be allowed to feel what they feel. Sometimes, just letting them know that we have noticed their feelings, *without trying to change the way they feel,* can help them feel better.

To feel good about themselves they need to know that even their strong or uncomfortable feelings like anger and jealousy are natural, and that they are not 'bad' because they feel that way.

Noticing our children's feelings

Here are some examples of how we can help our children when they are upset by letting them know that we have noticed their feelings.

A child came home from school upset because her teacher had accused her of spilling the art inks over the table, which she hadn't done. Her father said:

I just listened quietly, and when she'd told me, I said 'it sounds as if that really upset you'. She burst into tears, telling me how unfair it was, and that the person who had done it never owned up. She said she'd been feeling so bad about it that she hadn't even wanted to play with her friends at dinner time. After crying for a few minutes she calmed down, said she felt better now, and went off to call for her friend.

This might seem as if the father noticing his daughter's feelings made her feel worse; but actually she needed to let her feelings out before she could feel better.

Children can get very upset about things that seem like nothing to us. If we can remember what it felt like to be a child, and how important some things seemed, we might understand our children better.

My three-year-old was getting really cross because she couldn't fit the pieces of a puzzle together. She was starting to cry and I could see her becoming quite tense. I said 'You're annoyed because you can't do that'. She let out a loud yell and then seemed much better and finished the puzzle off. Before, I might have said 'Come on, it's only a puzzle' and she probably would have taken it all apart angrily, thrown the pieces around and cried for ages.

Getting ready in the morning can be a problem for a lot of families.

This particular day my son was doing everything possible to avoid getting ready for school – he wouldn't clean his teeth, spent ages sorting his bag out, and couldn't find his comb. I usually completely lose my temper by this stage, but that day I remembered to say what he was feeling. I said 'You really don't want to go to school today'. He said a very loud 'No! I don't', got his stuff together and went.

Sometimes children seem to need us to notice how they are feeling before they can talk about their problems.

After we moved house, my son took quite a while to settle into his new school. He didn't say anything about it, just looked a bit miserable, and seemed at a loose end. One day after a couple of weeks he was moping around while I was cooking, and I just said to him 'I expect you've been feeling lonely without your old friends'. It was like opening the flood gates – he talked for about half an hour about what he missed, why the new school wasn't as good as the old one, how hard it was because all the other boys already had friends, and so on. And I noticed that within a few days he seemed to be getting happier; about a week later he plucked up courage to invite someone round to play.

Painful feelings are a fact of life, and it's natural for parents to want to make their children's pain go away. But if we try to make it better by telling them not to worry, or not to feel that way, they may hide their feelings, which is likely to make matters worse. When we let them have their feelings, as in the examples above, they are more likely to get the feelings out and so feel better.

A FATHER: *My child threw a tantrum when I woudn't buy him a toy. I realised I felt upset as well, because I would have liked him to have it. So I told him: 'I feel sad that you're so upset; and I can't afford to buy it, so I can't let you have it.' He had one more outburst, then got the message and started to calm down.*

Helping our children say what they feel

Letting our children *have* their feelings is not the same as accepting what they might *do* about their feelings. The feeling and what we do about it are two different things.

There are many ways of saying how we feel. Some are safe and others cause problems. Feelings do need to come out one way or another, and one of our jobs is to help children express their feelings safely.

Here are some examples of how we could tell children that their feelings are OK but what they have done about it is not. At the same time we could offer them another way to express their feelings:

- 'It's alright to be angry but not to kick the cat. You can shout and stamp instead.'

- 'I know you're cross but that doesn't make it alright to scribble on your sister's homework. Tell her how you feel instead.'

- 'Even though you were jealous, drawing on your brother's new trainers was out of order. If you feel jealous I want you to talk about it.'

If we can help our children to *say* what they feel, or to find ways of showing their feelings without hurting others or doing any damage, both they and we (and the cat!) might have an easier time.

Dealing with our own feelings

Children are not the only ones who have strong feelings. Adults also need ways of letting their feelings out safely rather than bottling them up.

Here are some ways we can help ourselves with our strong feelings:

- tell a friend about them. For instance, just saying 'I felt so upset when I didn't get that job!' can help us feel better

- if we're tired and irritable when we come in from work, instead of taking this out on our children we could say: 'I'm really tired. I need ten minutes peace and quiet before I can do anything else.'

- if it feels hard to tell someone else, we can tell ourselves! Saying to ourselves 'I'm feeling under a lot of pressure' can make the feeling weigh on us less.

- take a few deep breaths and tell ourselves that even though we might not like what we're feeling, we're not bad for feeling that way

For many people, anger is the hardest feeling to cope with, and it can be the most dangerous when we don't know how to deal with it safely.

Parents and anger

Most parents love their children very much. For many of us our children are the centre of our lives, and we would do anything to protect them from harm. And yet, our children can also spark off levels of anger that we may rarely have felt before we had them.

Anger towards our children can be set off by fairly small things – clothes left all over the bathroom floor, a child refusing to clean teeth – as well as more important things like discovering that our child has been stealing, or that she or he had a party and wrecked the house while we were away. It can be useful to look at what our own anger tends to be triggered by, and how we deal with it.

WHAT MAKES YOU ANGRY WITH YOUR CHILDREN?

What sort of things do you tend to get angry at?
For example: *your children fighting, leaving a mess, lying to you*

Are there any situations, times of day, or other situations to do with you, rather than your children, when you are more likely to get angry?
For example: *when you come in from work, just before your period, around tea-time*

What are the different ways you show your anger?
For example: *by shouting, smacking, stomping around, going silent*

What do you think about being angry? Is it OK to get angry with your children, or do you think you are wrong or bad?

Parents often feel guilty about getting angry at their children. But anger is a natural emotion that we all feel. Getting angry does not mean we are bad parents, that we don't love our children, or that there's something wrong with us or them. It is a normal, natural part of being a parent. Sometimes it's because we have such love and high hopes for our children, that we can feel such anger.

Here are some ideas you might try, to help you deal with your anger without taking it out on your children:

- when you feel so angry that you are about to hit a child, go into another room. Tell your child what you're doing. For example, you might say 'I'm so angry. I'm going into the kitchen until I've calmed down.'

- *do* something – beat on a bed or sofa, stomp around, go for a fast walk or tear up paper. Anger is physical and often needs to come out physically. If you're disabled you may have to be creative about showing anger in a way that is safe for you but still releases the energy

- say loudly and clearly what you feel. For instance, 'I'm so angry about this!' (not 'You make me feel angry')

- wait until you've calmed down to decide what to do or say if your child has behaved badly. When we act in the heat of anger we do and say things that we wouldn't if we had thought about it.

Some ways we can stop ourselves getting angry

If you know the times you are most likely to get angry, try to avoid them. For example, if possible, try to make sure you get ten minutes to wind down when you get in from work before starting to do things for the children. If you've had a bad day get it out of your system by talking with a friend. Or if you get angry when you're hungry make sure you get a snack.

We've looked at the importance of getting our own needs met. The more we feel our needs are *not* being met, the more likely we are to get angry. Or we may, if we are that sort of person, just get depressed instead. Either way, getting our own needs met will help!

CHAPTER 5   Setting limits

What are boundaries?

Children need to know what kind of behaviour is allowed, or not allowed. They need to know where they stand, how far they can go. One of our jobs as parents is to set limits, or boundaries, for our children. This helps to keep them safe and teaches them what behaviour is allowed. If we don't set boundaries the chances are our children will run rings around us and other people.

Why we need boundaries

Boundaries are like fences on a farm. One reason for a fence is to keep animals safe by stopping them from wandering onto roads or off the edge of a cliff. Another is to stop the animals from causing damage to crops in the next field, or from being a danger to the public. Fences need to be strong to do their job properly.

Most of the time, animals stay well within the fence, but sometimes they push against it, and it might break. The farmer must then get the animals back in and fix the fence. But if the fence shuts in too small an area, the animals suffer by not having enough space. Eventually they will try to break out, and a new fence, around a larger field, will have to be put up.

Like fences, the boundaries we set for our children are needed for several reasons:

- **Safety**: some boundaries are for keeping children safe, and making them feel safe – actual boundaries such as stair gates when they are young, or a time to come in when they are teenagers.

- **Security**: to feel secure, children need to know what behaviour is OK. If they don't have firm boundaries they can feel unsafe. If there are no boundaries, children may behave in more and more extreme ways in order to get a reaction.

- **Something to push against:** it is normal for children to test boundaries by going beyond them, in order to find out what the rules really are. Sometimes, especially with older children, boundaries shift and need to be agreed all over again.

- **Discipline:** setting clear limits, for instance by saying 'NO!', is a way of teaching children what behaviour is allowed.

- **Self-discipline:** children need to learn *self*-discipline, that is setting limits on their own behaviour. Setting firm boundaries, especially if we get their agreement, helps them learn self-discipline, which helps them do well in life later on.

- **Personal boundaries:** these are the limits we have on how others may treat us. For example, a personal boundary might be that other people don't borrow our things without asking, or that they are not violent towards us. When our children learn to respect other people's boundaries, they also learn that *they* have personal boundaries too, which they can expect others to respect.

A PARENT: *My children have always been early risers. As soon as they were old enough we made a rule that they don't wake us up or make a lot of noise before 7.30, and 8.00 at weekends (except in an emergency, of course!). I've been really pleased that they've kept to it, apart from a very few occasions. They've learned from experience that neither of us are very nice to be around if we haven't had enough sleep – maybe that's helped!*

For boundaries to work, they need to be firm. Children need to know that the limit is the limit. Children will of course go too far sometimes. When they do, it's important that we make it clear again what the limit is, without being too angry about it. Children who walk all over their parents may need firmer boundaries. Later in this chapter we will look at how to be 'assertive' – giving clear boundaries *without* being aggressive.

As well as setting boundaries for our children's sake, to keep them safe or teach them what's OK, we need them to behave within certain limits for **our** sakes. Our personal boundaries are important too, and need to be respected.

Boundaries can change

Not all the limits we set are long-term rules. For instance, when we say 'No, you can't have another biscuit before tea' we are setting a limit. Although the limit is only for now, it's just as important that we are firm about it.

As children grow, we need to change the boundaries we have set. Our children can often be ahead of us in knowing what's right for them, as this father found out:

> *My teenage daughter was getting very angry that I wasn't allowing her to stay out after dark. It was only when she really pushed me that I realised that actually she was old enough to look after herself now, and that I'd been hanging on to a boundary that wasn't right for her any more.*

It's not always easy as a parent to know when our children have outgrown a boundary. We might think they are being naughty if they suddenly start refusing to go to bed at a certain time, for instance. But this might be their way of telling us that the old rule is no longer right for them, and that a new boundary – or bed-time – needs to be set. As children get older, it is possible to negotiate new boundaries with them.

What are some of the boundaries you have set for your children?
For instance: *no playing in the car park; no playing loud music at the weekend*

What were the reasons behind these boundaries when you set them?
For example: *to keep the children safe; to keep the neighbours happy*

Which ones work or have worked?
That is, did they keep the children safe, or the neighbours happy? Did the children stick to the rules?

If some have not worked, why do you think that is?
For example: *perhaps they were too strict or perhaps you found them difficult to insist on?*

What do you find hard about setting limits or keeping to them?
For example: *knowing whether a rule is fair, or what to do when the limits are broken*

Are there any new boundaries you would like to apply to your children's behaviour, either for their good or your own?

Are there any boundaries you set because you thought you ought to, and would like to remove now?

Where's the limit?

Children might also push at the boundaries we have set just to find out how firm the limits are, or because they want to be allowed to do what their friends do. It's important not to let boundaries be dropped *just* because our children want it that way, or because 'Everyone else is allowed to...' As the parent, it is up to you to decide which boundaries to set.

Boundaries can be flexible. We may not mind our children swearing at home, but we might insist that they keep their language clean elsewhere. We may have rules about when our children are allowed sweets; perhaps only after meals, or only at the weekend.

Too many boundaries

Although having firm boundaries is good for children it is possible to go overboard with them. Too many boundaries, or ones that are not needed any longer, can stifle children. Children need plenty of freedom *within* certain limits, to develop, to express themselves and to find out for themselves what feels right.

A GRANDMOTHER:

I was brought up very strictly. I realise now that nearly all of the battles I used to have with my own children were because I'd made too many rules. It was the only way I knew at the time, but I wish I'd known then what I know now. I'm glad my son has learnt the lesson and only has rules for his children that are really necessary.

When children have too many boundaries, their world can seem very negative. They are likely to have clashes with their parents and be very rebellious. The job for us is to find the balance between too many and too few boundaries.

> ### *Kids* by Spike Milligan
>
> 'Sit up straight'
> said Mum to Mabel.
> 'Keep your elbows
> off the table.
> Do not eat peas
> Off a fork.
> Your mouth is full –
> Don't try to talk.
> Keep your mouth shut
> When you eat.
> Keep still or you'll
> Fall off your seat.
> If you want more
> You will say "please".
> Don't fiddle with
> That piece of cheese!'
> If then we kids
> Cause such a fuss,
> Why do you go on
> Having us?

Making up our own minds

This book is not going to tell you what boundaries you *ought* to set, though one obvious one to suggest would be not harming other people. Here are some of the things we might allow for when we set limits on our children's behaviour:

- the child's age and stage of development

- our own cultural background

- our own personal values and beliefs

- the needs of the rest of the family

- where we live – safety factors could differ a great deal between an inner city and a country setting

When we are trying to decide what rules to set, it can be useful to think about what we want to achieve. If we set a boundary about something, who will get something out of it? What do we want our children to learn from it? Are we feeling pressured into it from outside? Do we feel really comfortable with it – if not we probably won't be able to insist on it.

Think about your own feelings about setting boundaries.

Do you find it easy or hard?

If you find it hard, what exactly is it that's hard?

Do you think you have the right to set limits on your children's behaviour?

Did your parents set limits on your behaviour?

How did they do it?

Remember, if it's painful to think about your own childhood, it's OK not to talk about it in the group. You may want to find someone else you trust to talk about it with.

Saying 'no'

A FATHER: *I used to wonder why my children never took any notice when I said 'no'. They always listened when their mother said 'no'. One day one of them actually told me that when I said 'no' it always sounded like 'maybe'. I try to say 'no' as if I really mean it now, but it's very hard.*

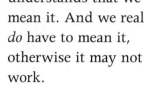

One of the best ways of setting a clear boundary, especially with very young children, is to say a firm *No*. Saying 'no' doesn't have to mean saying it loudly or aggressively. In fact, one of the best ways of saying 'no' is to get down to a child's level, look at her or him, and say it calmly and softly, but firmly, so that he or she really understands that we mean it. And we really *do* have to mean it, otherwise it may not work.

**Agreeing boundaries
with our children**

Often the boundaries that work best are those that our children have had some part in making. Finding limits that both we and they think are OK can be hard, but is often worth the effort. For instance, we may want them to do homework before watching TV, but they may not want to. By talking it through we might agree on a rule that they watch for no more than half an hour before they do their homework.

Styles of behaviour

There are three main ways of behaving and communicating, and most of us use a mixture of them. They are: **aggressive** behaviour, **passive** behaviour, and **assertive** behaviour

AGGRESSIVE

These are common **aggressive** ways of behaving:

- threatening people, either with words, or by tone of voice, or body language

- being willing to get something at any cost

- paying no attention to what other people need or want

- acting violently

- using put-downs, either seriously or with 'humour'

- saying things like 'you're a waste of time', 'you're hopeless' or 'don't be so stupid'.

PASSIVE

Passive behaviour (also called 'submissive') is the other side of the coin. People behaving passively:

- do not say what they need, want or think

- have an apologetic manner, as if they don't really have a right to be here

- don't stand up for themselves or think that their own feelings matter

- put other people's needs before their own, so that they don't get their own needs met

- use a quiet, weak tone of voice and don't often make eye contact with others

- put themselves down

- say things like 'I'm sorry to be such a nuisance', 'don't listen to me, I'm stupid' or 'I don't mind what we do, whatever you like is fine.'

ASSERTIVE   **Assertive** behaviour is quite different from both of these. When someone behaves assertively, they are clear about what they need or want, and are happy to say so. At the same time, they think about other people's needs, and try to make sure everyone gets what they need. They are at ease with themselves. They know that we are all as important as each other. They are more likely to be in touch with their own feelings, and care about other people's feelings. They don't steamroller over others, or play the doormat, like people behaving aggressively or passively.

Thankfully, very few people are totally aggressive or passive – most of us are a mixture. The more assertive we can be, the more we can get out of life.

Here are examples of these ways of responding applied to a situation in which a child has eaten all the biscuits after we have made it clear he or she can only have two:

- **aggressively** – smacking the child and shouting.

  The trouble with this is that it *won't* be likely to teach children not to do it next time. They are more likely to feel hurt and angry because they've been attacked. They are unlikely to want to do what we say in future.

- **passively** – saying something like 'Oh well, I don't suppose it really matters. Maybe you didn't realise you were eating so many. I can buy some more.'

  When children hear this, they not only get the message that it really doesn't matter, but are also likely to think that boundaries *never* matter.

- **assertively** – saying 'I'm really annoyed that you've eaten all those biscuits after I told you clearly that you could only have two. There are none left now for the rest of us. I want to know that next time you'll only take what you're allowed.'

  Hearing this, children are more likely to want to co-operate. They get a clear message about the effect of their behaviour on others. They haven't been attacked. And they know what we expect of them.

Of course, this makes it all sound simpler that it really is! Being assertive can take a lot of practice, and old habits die hard. But there are tricks that we can learn that can help us break these old habits.

Saying 'I' instead of 'You'

A big part of being assertive is letting others know how we feel and what we want, clearly, and in a way that respects them. One of the best ways to do this is to start what we say with the word 'I'. Here are some examples of how we could use this way of talking, when setting limits for our children, or when they have gone too far:

'I want you to put your toys away now.'

'I don't like what you're doing.'

'I told you yesterday that you could not use the car. I'm furious that you used it.'

'I'm fed up with you not bringing the mugs down from your room so that we end up with no clean ones.'

'I'm not going to let you do that.'

'I'm really angry about this!'

'I want you to feed the dog before you go out, as you agreed.'

Another important part of being assertive is respecting the other person's point of view. An assertive attitude would be 'This is what I think. What do you think?' Or 'How can we both get what we need?'

The problem with smacking

Smacking does not teach children how to behave. When they are hurt and humiliated, children are more likely to feel angry than sorry. And a smack may not stop them from doing it again, or help them to understand what they should have done, or how to put things right.

Smacking can be dangerous. Even a 'little tap' can cause a child to fall over and get really hurt, and a hard hit on the head or a shake can cause brain damage. Mild smacks can turn into serious beatings without the parent really meaning to go that far. And, as well as causing physical harm, smacking can make children feel bad about themselves.

Perhaps most important is what message children get when we hit them. Children learn most by copying our example. So when we smack them we are teaching that it's alright to hit people to get them to do what we want, especially when they are smaller than we are.

Research shows that children who are hit are much more likely to be violent both as children and when they grow up, than children who are not hit. If we want a less violent world, we can help by bringing up our children without using violence.

One of the aims of this book is to help you make changes if you want to, not to make you feel guilty. Most of us have been doing the best we could with what we knew at the time. Trying to change can be difficult at first, but with practice things get easier.

Positive discipline – what we can do instead of smacking

When we use 'positive discipline' we pay more attention *to the behaviour we like and want;* this works better for our children than paying attention to the behaviour we don't like.

Here are some ways to teach children through positive discipline:

- tell them what you want them to do, rather than what you don't want them to do

- say 'yes' and 'well done' at least as often as you say 'no' and 'don't do that'

- praise your children more often than you criticise them.

- reward your children with smiles, hugs and attention, rather than punishing them with smacks and yells

- when they do something you don't like, explain what it is and how they can put it right

- even though you may dislike what your child does, don't suggest you dislike your child

The more positive we are with our children, the more positive they will be with us. However, very few of us can change overnight. One of the problems with smacking is that it can become something we do without thinking. We need to allow ourselves time to learn new ways. We need to be patient with ourselves as well as our children.

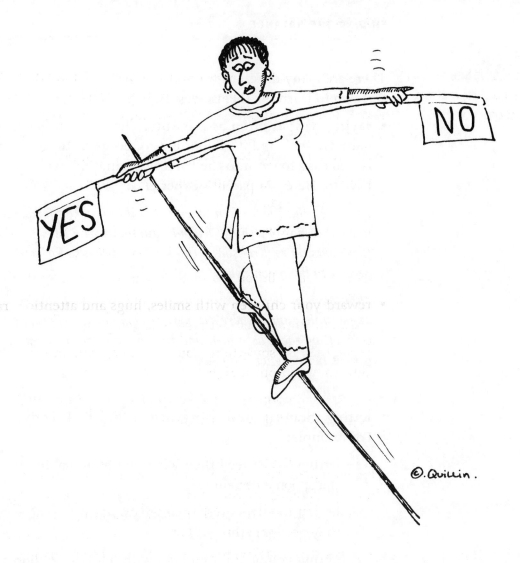

©.Quillin.

CHAPTER 6   Finding the balance

Control or freedom?

One of the things parents sometimes worry about is how much to control their children, and how much freedom to give them.

A certain amount of control by the parent or carer makes children safe and secure, helps them learn to discipline themselves, and teaches them important lessons about how to behave. We can provide all this by setting firm limits, which we discussed in chapter 5.

If we control children too much however, we are likely to end up with fights on our hands, for we're not giving them enough space to be themelves and do things their way.
Not allowing a young child to run free in the park, for example, might be too much control, and they could feel very restricted.
But letting them to run out of sight where they might get into danger could be too much freedom.

There are many different ways of giving our children more freedom to learn for themselves. Here are some:

- **saying 'yes' as often as possible.** There are times when we must say 'no', and it's important to recognise those times. But it is also easy to get into the habit of saying 'no' when you don't have to. Here is a parent's experience:

I realised that very often when my children asked for something or wanted to do something, I would automatically say 'no', even when there was no real reason. I think it was because for some reason I needed to be in control.

Now I try to do it the other way round, so that I say 'yes' as often as possible, unless there's a good reason not to. This way I'm not controlling them as much, and they have more freedom. They also take it better when I do say 'no'.

- **letting them try new things when they feel ready.**
  For example:

  - letting babies feed themselves, without making them hold the spoon a certain way

  - letting toddlers dress themselves, not worrying whether they get everything right

  - letting young children help with household chores

  - letting older children go on public transport on their own

  - letting teenagers experiment with styles of dress you might not approve of

While it is good to trust our children's judgement about when they are ready to do new things, we need to use our own judgement as well if safety issues are involved (for instance when a child wants to use sharp knives).

Like adults, children will often not do a brilliant job the first few times they try something, and they may take longer than we would. This can be frustrating for us, but it will be good for all of us in the end if we can still let them do it.

This doesn't mean we should not give help if they want it! Giving help when they ask for it shows that we trust them to know what they need.

- **letting them do things their own way.** Our children may find ways of doing things that are not our own. If we let them know that this is alright, they will learn that they don't have to be the same as us to get our approval.

- **organising our homes so our children have more control.** Sometimes children cannot do the things they want to because of practical problems. Here are some examples of how we might help:

    - giving toddlers a chair to stand on so they can stir the cake

    - storing games and puzzles at a height that our children can reach so they don't have to ask when they want them

    - having low pegs for children's coats

- **suggesting new things they might not have thought of.** Sometimes a little bit of help can go a long way in helping our children to do more for themselves.

Jordan was making a den with furniture and old sheets. He was getting really cross because the den kept collapsing. I suggested he could try using clothes pegs to hold the sheets onto the chairs. He then spent hours making dens and spaceships of all different shapes and sizes. Now he uses pegs in other ways as well – for instance holding cardboard boxes together and making dressing up outfits. That simple idea has given him hours of fun.

- **letting them learn from their own experience and mistakes.** For instance:

    - letting a toddler keep building a tower till it falls down will let the toddler learn how to judge when the tower is getting too high to stand up

    - if you have arguments with your child about wearing gloves or a hat when it's cold, you could stop insisting. The child will either learn that he or she gets cold, and take them next time, or won't mind the cold – so there's no problem

    - refusing to replace a toy that went rusty because it was left outside will teach a child about looking after things

    - not picking up your children's dirty clothes when they are going to want them for the disco will teach them to put them in the wash-basket themselves

    Of course, this doesn't mean that we should *always* let our children learn from experience. Letting them learn from experience what happens if they walk onto a busy road is not such a good idea!

- **offering choices.** We can help our children get better at making decisions and be more independent by offering choices rather than telling them what to do. For example, we might:

    - offer a young child a choice between eggs or sausages for tea. (An older child could help think up a whole week's meals)

    - give choices about the clothes we buy them

    - let them make their own choices at the library

- **helping them follow up their interests.** When children show an interest in something new, encourage them as much as you can. There is nothing wrong with children being interested in things that may be thought of as typical of the other sex (for instance, a boy playing with dolls, or a girl wanting to learn football). It's important not to make children feel bad for this.

- **letting them make their own decisions, right for their age.**
  When children are a certain age we might change our mind
  about who makes decisions on:
    - how or whether to have their hair cut

    - whether our children need a bath

    - how often they practise their musical instruments

    - whether they get their ears pierced

    - how they spend their money

- **giving them a feeling of responsibility.** We can help children
  become more independent by letting them do more for themselves as they grow up. For instance, at different ages we might
  expect them to:
    - clean their teeth without being told

    - look after their own pets

    - buy their own clothes

But it's also important not to make them do so much for
themselves that they can't enjoy just being children.

When we let our children learn for themselves we are showing
them that we believe in them, and trust them to find their own
ways, which may not be the same as ours.

Some of us like to have more control. This is especially likely if we
were strictly controlled when we were children. Others of us find it
a bother to always tell our children what to do, but we're worried
that if we don't control them they may run wild. Often we're not
even aware of whether we're controlling our children or not.

The more we become aware of how we are trying to control them,
the easier it gets to find the right balance.

Think of a time when you let your child learn something for him or herself instead of controlling the situation

What was the child doing?

What did you do or not do that let them learn for themselves, rather than control them?

Can you think of a situation in which you usually control your child when there's no real need? Such as: *making decisions that they could make, insisting they do something a certain way, saying 'no' when you could say 'yes'.*

What could you do instead that would give them more freedom to learn for themselves?

How do you feel about letting go of some of the control you have over your children?

If you don't feel happy about it, can you think why not?
What might happen if your children had more control?

Saying what we like

As we saw in chapter 5, we can make life more positive both for ourselves and our children by saying what we do like rather than what we don't. Telling them what we like also helps children feel good about themselves. For instance, we could say:

- 'I like how you left your room tidy yesterday'

- 'You came in at exactly the time we agreed'

- 'You've been doing a really good job of looking after the hamster'

- 'I liked how you shared your toys when your friend came round to play'

Children and adults need other people's approval. When we show our approval by saying positive things about our children's behaviour, it makes them want to behave that way again.

EXERCISE

Think of at least one positive thing you could say about each of your children, and agree with yourself to say it to them this week. It could be about something they've done recently, or about how they are generally.

Write here what you could say to each child.

Saying what we want

Saying what we want instead of what we don't want is another way of making life more positive. And because it helps children see just what we expect of them *it can be a better way of getting the behaviour we want* than telling them what *not* to do.

For example, we could say:

- 'Stay on the pavement' instead of 'don't go on the road'.
- 'Try to keep your food on the plate' instead of 'don't make such a mess'.
- 'I want this room tidy by tea-time'

EXERCISE

Think of a positive way of saying each of these statements:

You can't go out till you've finished your homework.

Stop making such a noise in here.

Don't leave those sweet wrappers all over the place.

Don't spend all night on the phone again.

A MOTHER: *I think the best tip anyone ever gave me about looking after children was about asking for what I want rather than what I don't want. It was such a simple idea and makes all the difference – life just feels better – more positive. I say things like 'please keep quiet in there' and 'walk with me' instead of 'stop the racket' and 'don't dawdle'.*

CHAPTER 7   Being a parent can be fun!

As parents, we can learn a lot from our children about having fun. We may not have been allowed to play much when we were children ourselves, or we may have grown up to think that adults shouldn't play. This is not true! Adults need fun and relaxation as much as children do.

Some psychologists say that all of us still have a child inside us, however old we are. They call this our 'inner child'. Even after we have become parents, this inner child still wants to play and have fun; we can do ourselves a lot of good by listening to our inner child, and by having fun, in whatever way feels right to us.

Doing things together

As well as being fun, doing things together can be good both for us and our children. We can get to know them better and get more of an idea of how they see the world. They like it when we play with them because they are getting our attention and getting the message that we like being with them.

When we are playing or even just talking with children, it's a good idea to get down to their level, if we can, so that we are facing one another. (If we can't get down to their level we might be able to get them up to ours, by letting them stand on a chair for example).

It can be quite frightening to have to look up to someone who's much bigger than us, as many adults know. Being at the same level gives more of an equal feel to our relationship. And seeing the world from their point of view can be quite an eye-opener for us.

If we feel guilty about all the things we think we 'ought' to be doing instead of spending time playing with our children, we can tell ourselves how much good it's doing us and them. The more we do it, the happier our families will be.

Of course, if we don't enjoy our time with them we are likely to resent it, so it's important to choose things to play together that both or all of us will enjoy.

Here are some ways we can have fun with young children that we might not have done since we were children ourselves, if ever:

- play with playdough – just messing about, not expecting great works of art. Making things with clay or dough can be very relaxing

- join them in painting – again just trying things out in a child-like way can be good for us

- play 'let's pretend' with them – it can be fun to swap roles so they play at being a parent and we're the child. We might learn something about how they see us!

- play ball games

With older children the things we can do with them aren't always really 'playing', but they can be just as rewarding. For instance:

- talking with them about their interests, what they are reading, what they think about things, what's going on at school or with their friends

- going for bike rides or swimming

- playing board games

DOING THINGS WITH YOUR CHILDREN

Think about the different ways your children play. Did you play like that when you were a child?

Of the different ways your children play, which do you think you would enjoy?

If you don't do many things with your children, can you imagine what it might feel like?

Is there anything that would make it hard for you to do things with them?

(You may already spend plenty of time playing with your children – if so you might like to use this exercise to think of even more ways of getting involved with them.)

Making time to be with them is one of the most important things we can do for our children. Making it fun for ourselves is one of the most important things we can do for us!

More on listening

We've already seen how much we can help our children just by listening to them.

In chapter 2 we talked about quiet listening – simply paying attention and letting children know we are with them by saying things like'mmm' and 'oh'. When we listen quietly to someone the other person knows that we care for them. We are supporting them – giving them the space to talk through their problem, and perhaps begin to find an answer .

In chapter 4 we talked about naming our children's feelings as we listen to them – for instance, by saying 'you sound upset' or 'I expect that hurt your feelings'. This can help our children because it lets them know that we accept their feelings – that even when their feelings are painful, they are not bad for feeling that way.

Naming feelings can also help calm someone who is upset. Then they are in a better position to sort out whatever the problem is that's made them feel that way.

What might get in the way of listening

However much we want to help our children by listening when they have a problem, sometimes we are just not in the right state of mind. Most of us probably know what it feels like to talk to someone about something that's important to us, and it turns out that they are not really listening at all. We can end up wishing that we hadn't spoken to them.

If we are just too busy to give enough time, or if we are feeling upset or annoyed by what's going on, then we probably won't be able to give our children proper attention. In that case it is usually better not to try to listen. So that our children don't think we're not interested, we could explain that we do want to hear about it, but not until later when we can give them the attention they deserve.

WHAT MAKES IT HARD FOR YOU TO LISTEN?

Are there any particular times when it's harder for you to listen to your children?

How do you feel when your children want to talk at those times?

Are there other times when you could listen to them?

What could you say so they know that you care ?

Helping our children talk

When someone has a problem, they might want to talk about it but not really know how to get started. Or they might get stuck when they're talking and not know how to go on.

We can help by asking questions to get them started or to help them move on, if they want to. You might like to try some of the following:

- door-openers – these are phrases, or even single words, that might get your children talking. For instance:

  Feeling upset about something?

  Angry?

  If you want to talk, I'm here.

  Do you want to talk about it?

- phrases which might help your children to keep talking, if they want to. For example:

What happened next?

Can you tell me more?

This seems important; tell me the whole story.

It sounds like something else is going on.....

And then...?

Asking questions when someone is very upset isn't very helpful, because they can't think straight enough to answer. It's usually better to wait until they've got their strong feelings out (for instance by crying), and to help them calm down by naming their feelings, before we try to find out what happened.

The difference between open and closed questions

If we ask questions when we're listening, we can be more helpful if we use open questions, such as 'How did it happen?' rather than closed questions such as 'Did he push you over?'

This is because open questions let children talk about what's on *their* mind; that way, they are more likely to sort out the problem, or at least get the problem off their chest.

Closed questions either get a yes or no answer, which can stop the flow of conversation, or lead the child in a certain direction, which may not be the most helpful for them.

Here are some examples of closed and open questions:

closed: *Were you rude to your teacher?*
open: *That sounds bad. What happened?*

closed: *Have you been in trouble again?*
open: *You're a bit late home today. What happened?*

closed: *Have those girls been leaving you out again?*
open: *You seem upset. Do you want to tell me about it?*

If we are not used to listening as a way of helping, it can feel strange to start with, but it gets easier. Quiet listening, and letting children know we've noticed their feelings is often enough to help them when they are upset. Adding open questions is really an optional extra, once we've got used to quiet listening.

Review of the course

We've covered a lot of ground on this course. Having reached the end, this is a chance to think about what you've got out of it, and whether you want to go further. Here's a reminder of the main things we've covered:

- what it's *really* like being a parent – how life changes when we become parents, and how we change as parents as our children grow up – what is hard and what fun about being a parent

- why parents are important – noticing and liking what we do well – looking after ourselves and having fun – how a parenting group can help

- the most valuable things we can do for our children – especially how we can help them feel good about themselves

- how we can help our children by listening to them when they are upset or have a problem

- why feelings are important – accepting our own and our children's feelings – how we can help ourselves and our children with feelings – coping with our angry feelings

- how what we do is a way of getting our needs met – thinking about behaviour as OK or not OK, rather than 'good' or 'bad'

- describing our children's *behaviour* rather than giving *children themselves* a label (such as *naughty*)

- how to make life more positive – telling our children what we like about what they do, and asking for what we want rather than saying what we don't want

- setting limits – why children need to have limits – how to set limits

- the difference between aggressive, passive and assertive behaviour – how to be assertive – starting sentences with 'I'

- the trouble with smacking

- giving our children enough freedom to learn for themselves – letting them learn from their mistakes and make their own decisions

- why children need to play – what they learn from different sorts of play

COURSE REVIEW EXERCISE

What are the most important or useful things you have learnt from the course?

Has anything changed in your family as a result?

How do you think you've changed as a parent? For instance, has your attitude towards your children's behaviour changed? Or to their play?

What do you want to find out more about?

What support do you need?

Getting more support

If you feel that this course has helped you, you might want to consider forming a support group with some or all of the other parents, to continue meeting. Many of us have found that continuing to meet helps us make the most of what we've learned on a course. A support group offers us the chance to help and support each other and gives us a regular time away from the children to talk things through with other parents. It's also a chance to learn more about how we can help ourselves and our children, as our families grow and change.

Support groups can be of all different shapes and sizes; some get together weekly, some monthly, some less often. Some meet in someone's house, some in a cafe or a pub. Some decide in advance what they want to talk about, others see what comes up at the time. The details are up to the parents in the group, and what you feel you need.

If you and others from the course want to talk about forming a support group, your course leader will be happy to help you.

Parent Network also runs other courses for parents. Your group leader will be able to tell you about them, and about what's available in your area.

If you have enjoyed this one, you might like to think about going on to another.

APPENDIX Play Recipes

Recipe for playdough

Ingredients
100g plain white flour
1 tsp cream of tartar
50g salt
1 tsp cooking oil
150ml water
1-2 tsp food colouring

METHOD
1. Mix flour, salt, cream of tartar and oil in a saucepan. Stir well.
2. Add food colouring and stir well
3. Gradually add water, mix thoroughly to remove any lumps
4. Cook over low-medium heat, stirring continuously until dough becomes very thick and leaves sides of pan almost clean.
5. Scrape mixture from pan onto a smooth, flat surface. Put pan to soak immediately.
   Leave to cool at least 10 minutes.
6. Knead cooled dough until smooth and pliable.

STORAGE TIP
Roll into a ball and wrap in cling film, keep in an airtight container in the fridge. Will keep for months.

Cornflour paste

Cornflour is sold in small packets which can usually be found in any grocery store or supermarket.

Wet cornflour has an unusual feel and playing with it can give children hours of fun. The texture varies depending on how much water is added and it can be coloured with food colouring. If spilt, it is easily wiped up – any left will brush off when dry. Once made, the mixture can reconstituted by adding water next time you want to use it.

RECIPE
Put a few tablespoons of ordinary cornflour into a shallow dish. Gradually add a small amount of water, until you have a fairly thick, squeaky texture. Experiment with the amount of water you add for different textures. (If you add too much it will get too runny to be much use – but just save it till the next day and it will have thickened.)

Put on apron, roll up sleeves and dive in!

Recommended Reading

A Selection of Books for Parents

Books by Steve Biddulph:

Manhood
Hawthorn Press, Gloucestershire 1998, ISBN 1 8698 9099 X

Raising Boys
Thorsons, London 1998, ISBN 0 7225 3686 0

The Secret of Happy Children
Thorsons, London 1998, ISBN 0 7225 3669 0

Becoming A Father
Mike Lilley, How To Books, Plymouth ISBN 1 85703 327 2
How to make a success of your role as a father.

Communicating With Your Teenager
Sheila Munro, Piccadilly Press, London 1998 ISBN 1 85340 516 6

By the same author:
Overcome Bullying – for parents
Sheila Munro, Piccadilly Press, London 1997, ISBN 1 85340 490 X
A guide for parents to help children overcome bullying.

Coping With Loss
Pat Elliot, Piccadilly Press, London 1997, ISBN 1 85340 453 5
A guide for parents to help children cope with loss or separation.

How to Talk so Kids can Learn
Adele Faber and Elaine Mazlish, Rawson Associates NY 1982,
ISBN 0 684 81333 5
(For parents and teachers)

By the same authors:
How to Talk so Kids Will Listen and Listen so Kids Will Talk
Adele Faber and Elaine Mazlish, Avon Books, NY 1982,
ISBN 0 380 57000 9

Siblings Without Rivalry
Adele Faber and Elaine Mazlish, Piccadilly Press, London 1999,
ISBN 1 85340 630 9

Keeping Safe
Michelle Elliott, Coronet, London 1994, ISBN 0 340 624 825
Covers prevention of sexual abuse as well as safety tips for public places, good for all ages, including teenagers.

Kids can Co-operate, A Practical Guide to Teaching Problem Solving
Elizabeth Crary, Parenting Press Inc., 7750 31st Ave NE Seattle, WA 98115, USA

By the same author:
Pick up Your Socks, and Other Skills Growing Children Need
and
Without Spanking or Spoiling, A Practical Approach to Toddler and Pre-school Guidance
Excellent 'workbooks' which give a variety of approaches to try out.

Learning to Step Together: Building and Strengthening Stepfamilies
National Stepfamily Association, Tel: ParentLine 0808 800 2222

Parenting Matters
Hawthorn Press, Gloucestershire 1998, ISBN 1 8 698 90 16 7
Also available from Parent Network,
Tel. 0171 735 1214 [020 7735 1214]
Parenting Matters *is the workbook designed to support Parent Network's Parenting Matters course* (Understanding Children 2). *Packed with ideas, exercises and examples for personal use, it is useful for parents of children of all ages.*

Books for Children

All Kinds of People
Emma Damon, Discovery Personal Development Books, Freepost LON7858, London SE23 2BR.
This lift-the-flap book celebrates all kinds of children from different backgrounds and cultures.

Dinosaurs' Divorce
Laurene & Mark Brown, Discovery Personal Development Books, Freepost LON7858, London SE23 2BR.
A unique approach to exploring how families change and develop after a divorce. Totally accessible, child-centred approach, the dinosaurs' experiences help to ease children's fears and insecurities.

National Open College Network
Unit Information

Understanding Children 1

Entry Level   Credit Value 1   Unit Code 8931

Learning Outcomes	Assessment Criteria
On completion of this unit the Learner will know/understand/be able to:	The Learner has demonstrated the ability to:
1. Understand the value of being a parent.	1. State some of the difficulties of being a parent.
2. Appreciate oneself as a parent.	2. Give an example of something s/he does well as a parent.
3. Enjoy mutual support with other parents.	3. Talk and listen to other parents and share experiences in the group.
4. Participate in group observing ground rules.	4. Name and observe ground rules, (e.g. confidentiality).
5. Demonstrate group skills.	5. Use basic group skills of speaking in groups and listening to others.
6. Understand parenting roles.	6. List different roles within being a parent.
7. Understand the importance of accepting feelings and understand that feelings change.	7a. Accept feelings in others. 7b. Accept strong feelings in a child.
8. Help a child when upset by using listening skills.	8. Use listening skills.
9. Understand the value of play.	9. Take part in a play activity within the group.
10. Understand the needs of parent and child.	10a. State some basic needs of a child. 10b. State some of own needs as parents.

Learning Outcomes	Assessment Criteria
On completion of this unit the Learner will know/understand/be able to:	The Learner has demonstrated the ability to:
11. Make links between needs and behaviour.	11. Give an example of a child's behaviour resulting from an unmet need.
12. Understand the value of boundaries.	12. Say why children need boundaries.
13. Understand the difference between controlling and enabling a child.	13. State the difference between controlling and enabling a child.
14. Understand the difference between aggressive and assertive behaviour.	14. State the difference between aggressive and assertive behaviour.
15. Understand the difference between describing behaviour and 'labelling' a child.	15. Give an example of a 'label'.
16. Understand how to manage children's behaviour.	16. Give an example of acceptable and unacceptable behaviour.
17. Know where to obtain further support on parenting issues.	17. Use list provided of services and organisations that help parents.

Understanding Children 1

Level One   Credit Value 1   Unit Code 8932

Learning Outcomes	Assessment Criteria
On completion of this unit the Learner will know/understand/be able to:	**The Learner has demonstrated the ability to:**
1. Understand the value of being a parent.	1. State the value to children and society of being a parent.
2. Appreciate oneself as a parent.	2. Describe something s/he does well as a parent, and give reasons for choice.
3. Enjoy mutual support with other parents.	3. Give examples of experiences shared in the group and describe why it's useful to do this.
4. Participate in group, observing ground rules.	4. Describe some ground rules, and state why they are important.
5. Demonstrate group skills.	5. Communicate in group and 'own' opinions and feelings.
6. Understand parenting roles.	6. Describe some roles within being a parent.
7. Understand the importance of accepting feelings and understand that feelings change.	7a. State own feelings in group and accept feelings in others. 7b. Give example of child having strong feelings and how the feelings changed when the feelings were accepted.
8. Help a child when upset by using listening skills.	8. Give an example of when learner has helped a child using listening skills, and how the child was helped.
9. Understand the value of play.	9. Describe the value of play for children and give examples.
10. Understand the needs of parent and child.	10a. Describe some basic needs of a child. 10b. Describe some of the basic needs of a parent and give an example of a need being met.

Learning Outcomes	Assessment Criteria
On completion of this unit the Learner will know/understand/be able to:	The Learner has demonstrated the ability to:
11. Make links between needs and behaviour.	11a. Give an example of a child's behaviour resulting from an unmet need. 11b. Describe the effect on the behaviour of a child's needs being met.
12. Understand the value of boundaries.	12. Explain why children need boundaries and describe some ways of setting boundaries.
13. Understand the difference between controlling and enabling a child.	13. Give different examples of controlling and enabling a child.
14. Understand the difference between aggressive and assertive behaviour.	14a. Describe the difference between aggressive and assertive behaviour. 14b. Give an example of an assertive 'I' statement.
15. Understand the difference between describing behaviour and 'labelling' a child.	15a. Describe the difference between describing behaviour and 'labelling' a child. 15b. Give an example of describing behaviour.
16. Understand how to manage children's behaviour.	16a. Describe what is acceptable and unacceptable behaviour. 16b. Give an assertive message.
17. Know where to obtain further support on parenting issues.	17. Refer to list provided of services and organisations that help parents.

List of Exercises

OTHER BOOKS FROM HAWTHORN PRESS

HAWTHORN PRESS
Hawthorn House, 1 Lansdown Lane, Stroud, Gloucestershire GL5 1BJ
Tel: (01453) 757040 Fax: (01453) 751138
E-mail: hawthornpress@hawthornhouse.com

Distributor
Scottish Book Source, 137 Dundee Street, Edinburgh EH11 1BG
Tel: (0131) 229 6800 Fax: (0131) 229 9070

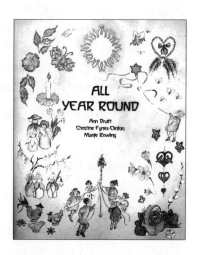

All Year Round

Ann Druitt, Christine Fynes-Clinton, Marije Rowling
Brimming with seasonal stories, activities, crafts, poems and
recipes, this book offers a truly inspirational guide to
celebrating festivals throughout the seasons.

288pp; 250 X 200mm; paperback; ISBN 1 869 890 47 7.

The Children's Year
CRAFTS AND CLOTHES FOR CHILDREN AND PARENTS TO MAKE

Stephanie Cooper, Christine Fynes-Clinton, Marije Rowling
You needn't be an experienced craftsperson to create beautiful
things! This charmingly illustrated book encourages children
and adults to try all sorts of different handwork, with projects
relating to the seasons of the year. Over 50,000 sold.

250 X 200mm; 192pp; paperback; ISBN 1 869 890 00 0.

Festivals, Family and Food
Diana Carey and Judy Large
An ideal companion to *Festivals Together,* this explores those
numerous annual 'feast days' which children love celebrating.
Over 100,000 copies sold.

250 X 200mm; illustrations; 216pp; paperback;
ISBN 0 950 706 23 X.

Festivals Together

A Guide to Multicultural Celebration

Sue Fitzjohn, Minda Weston, Judy Large

A resource guide for celebration, based on many cultures from all over the world – Buddhist, Christian, Hindu, Jewish, Muslim and Sikh.

250 X 200mm; 224pp; paperback; ISBN 1 869 890 46 9

Raising a Son

Parents and the Making of a Healthy Man

Don Elium and Jeanne Elium

Many parents feel frustrated and confused by the behaviour of their sons and are in need of some practical guidance. *Raising a Son* offers just that: advice on firm but fair discipline that will encourage the awakening of your son's healthy soul. U.S. best seller.

215 X 138mm; 256pp; paperback; ISBN 1 869 890 76 0

Games Children Play

How Games and Sport Help Children Develop

Kim Brooking-Payne

Illustrated by Marije Rowling

Games Children Play offers an accessible guide to games with children of age 3 upwards. These games are all tried and tested, and are the basis for the author's extensive teacher training work. The book explores children's personal development and how this is expressed in movement, play, songs and games.

Each game is clearly and simply described, with diagrams or drawings, and accompanied by an explanation of why this game is helpful at a particular age. The equipment that may be needed is basic, cheap and easily available.

297 X 210mm; 192pp; paperback; ISBN 1 869 890 78 7

Manhood

An action plan for changing men's lives

Steve Biddulph

Manhood is having a profound impact on the lives of men and women since publication in Australia. Well read copies are passed from hand-to-hand-by friends, partners, work mates, from sons to fathers – with the simple message, 'You must read this!'

This practical book is full of helpful insights, personal experiences and solutions. It is written for older men, young men, working men, unemployed men, business men, grandfathers, fathers and sons. It is also written for women who want to understand what helps and hinders men's growth. However, the responsibility is firmly put with men to work together for their own development.

Steve Biddulph is a family psychologist. He was born in Yorkshire and lives in Tasmania. He makes regular lecture tours to Britain. His books *Raising Boys, The Secret of Happy Children* and *More Secrets of Happy Children* have sold half a million copies in five languages.

216 X 138mm; 272pp; 12 black and white photos; paperback; ISBN 1 869 89 099 X

Many parents feel frustrated and confused by the behaviour of their sons and are in need of